My Sin

The glossy magazines for years have carried full-page ads for a perfume called "My Sin." I presume that they still do, but Lanvin perhaps knows that the name is now considered somewhat out-of-date. Sin is no longer considered so alluring or enticing—or even sophisticatedly wicked, for that matter.

My own sin of sorts is that two years ago I agreed to write a book about sin. Not a full theological treatise but some pastoral reflections on sin. And I never did get it written. Oh, I worked on it. And I read dozens of theological, biblical, and ethical works on the matter. I discovered that sin is a tiny word but a large subject. It is a thin little word. Not even a four-letter word. Just a little slip of a word, with a slightly nasal sound. It doesn't take much breath to say it.

Yet it would take many volumes to cover fully the topic of sin. One would have to go into the notion of sin as found in the Old and the New Testaments, the history of moral theology over the past 20 centuries of the church, and the fresh outlooks on sin and moral conduct explored in the new and numerous theological studies after Vatican Council II.

Such an exhausting project is not envisioned here. I intend only to make some pastoral reflections on some aspects of sin in answer to some questions asked of me.

Americans are a practical people. To their questions about the meaning of life they want practical answers. They want to know what to do. Many are concerned about the loss, as they see it, of a sense of morality when they see the word, or ideas of, sin passing out of our lives. They hear more about sinfulness, about being "authentically human," and hear other terminology about which they are uncomfortable because it seems vague.

Christ is sometimes thought of as being impractical. But he was a most practical person, practical in using the best means for his mission from the Father. Even his death on the cross was practical, for he would not have impressed the world without it.

People ask, "What happened to the idea of sin? What is a sin? Should we still learn the Ten Commandments? How do I know that I am sinning? What do I do about my sins?"

Actually, I do not like to write about sin. I would rather write about our life in God, about more cheerful topics, about the virtues (even though one writer on the spiritual life thinks we should drop the term). But we do commit sin, it is ever with us, and it is the most horrible and destructive thing in the world. It is something we should dread, a monster ever lurking in the shadows of our lives.

It is everywhere in the world and has been with us since the beginning of time. So we had better not close our eyes to its existence and we had better do something about it.

Something practical.

Has Sin Become Outmoded?

"Ma, what's a washboard?"

One day I heard a child ask his mother this question. It struck me as a dumb question at first, but then I realized that the child had been raised in the days of automatic washers and dryers and detergents. His mother certainly did not use that rectangular wooden frame with a corrugated metal surface over which clothes were rubbed while being washed. It was once a common household item in America.

The child might also have asked what a damper is, a boiler, a biplane, isinglass. A damper is a movable metal plate used for regulating draft in a chimney; a poker is a metal rod used for poking or stirring a fire, used in kitchen stoves; a boiler is an oblong tub, often made of copper, in which clothes were soaked in boiling hot water; a biplane is an airplane (aeroplane) with two sets of wings; and isinglass is the popular name for a form of mica used for the many small windows of the heater stoves burning hard coal.

But the way things are going, children may soon be asking people what a *sin* is. For sin seems to be joining the list of obsolete words. The reality of sin is still here; it has always been here. But the idea that there is evil for which a person is individually responsible seems to be passing out of existence. Sin is a word which is used almost as rarely today as washboard, clothes boiler, poker, biplane, isinglass.

To use the word dates a person. It almost makes a person out-of-date, one of the past generation. A sophisticate would hardly use the word except in derision. For some it is a silly word, a fun word, a word to be used in jokes by a "superior" person. We are embarrassed to use the word before a worldly-wise person.

WHAT IS SIN?

Sin, we soon learn, is not an easy word to define. We use many words and have many experiences that are not easy to define. Just try defining the word *love.* Yet love is something we have experienced and recognize, and we all have used the term. Sin also is something that we have experienced, that we do. When we freely do evil we are sinning. Since we do it freely, with full awareness of what we are doing, we are responsible for what we do and are accountable for it.

It seems, though, that the consciousness of sin is disappearing from human life. The concept of sin is something we no longer bother with. And thus we do evil and do not feel responsible for it. I have just read of a survey in which of the people polled 25 percent said that they would kill someone for $50,000. The conditions were that the killing would be done without discovery of the killer, without violence, and without personal knowledge of the victim.

As with so many sins, we think that we are getting by with it if we don't get caught. We forget what damage the sin does to ourselves and we forget God. With the growing loss of the concept of personal sin we are losing a sense of responsibility. As though we had to answer to no one. I do think that this is affecting very young people. More and more crimes are being committed by younger and younger people. We read of children torturing and even killing old, incapacitated people.

Watergate, of course, was no help to the young. Nor were the revelations of big business bribes and the crimes of such government agencies as the FBI and the CIA. Evil begets evil, and it gradually makes people cynical. No one wants to be a sucker for others. Gradually it becomes each one for oneself and we become a subhuman people living in greed, and the result is eventually a society of fear.

Disease of its very nature spreads, and so does the disease of moral evil. One thing that helps evil to spread is to sugarcoat it, to give it nice names. We now call the sin of stealing "ripping off" someone. It doesn't sound so bad that way. We give it a faddish word. Robbery on the street with a gun or knife we term "mugging." Somehow it does not sound so evil. And "making love" is often used in cases of sexual injustice or mere selfishness. I recall that in a moral theology class in the seminary one student referred to a serious moral violation as an "indiscretion."

"Indiscretion, hell!" slammed back the professor, "that is a sin!"

THE REMISSION OF SIN

I am not sure why the admission of sin is passing out of existence. Some people say that the advent of psychology has explained away all the causes of guilt. That we can be excused for our behavior because of our psychological makeup. (And "values-clarification" takes the place of moral guidance.) It is true that psychological insights help us understand our individual natures better and help us see that in some areas we have diminished culpability; but we still have a free will in most of our decisions.

St. Paul admits that "I do not do the good I want, but the evil I do not want is what I do" (Romans 7:19), but a better self-knowledge can also be a help in combatting sin. To eliminate all responsibility for sin is to eliminate the human in us, to reduce us to machines or vegetables, to take away our dignity as people of God.

I am not sure if the diminished sense of sin is responsible for the greatly decreased number of sacramental confessions, or if the decrease in sacramental confessions is responsible for the decreased sense of sin. It may be another case of the chicken or the egg. One reason, however, for the decline in the number of people "going to confession" is that many things were listed as sins which hardly deserved the term. People evidently caught on to this and they stopped going. However, they threw out the baby with the bath water.

9

For the real sins were still there, and Vatican Council II, along with modern theologians, tried to form consciences sensitive to the real evils we were committing. Over the 2000 years of the church's existence moral theologians dissected and analyzed and categorized our moral life and, having nothing else to do, came up with lists of sins so extensive and so detailed and with sins so minute and artificial that a Christian would become a nervous wreck trying to avoid them all. It was the very thing Christ had condemned in the Pharisees. Modern educated Christians would not accept this false sense of sin.

But they made the mistake of ending confession of real sins along with ending confession of false sins. Whether we admit them or not, the real sins are still with us. The first book of the Bible talks about sin and the last book of the Bible talks about it. The prophets told us to repent of our sins; John the Baptist did likewise, and so did Jesus Christ.

Luke ends his Gospel with Christ telling us that in Christ's name "penance for the remission of sins is to be preached to all nations." If there was no such thing as sin then Christ's mission, his teaching, suffering, and death were in vain, and he is the greatest fool that ever lived. At the consecration in the Mass we read that Christ's blood was shed for us "so that sins may be forgiven." If there is no such thing as sin, his blood was shed in vain. And we can forget about the Mass.

One more thing which may have contributed to the loss of the sense of sin today, or at least assisted us in taking a most mild view of sin, is the emphasis today on the merciful and loving nature of God our Father. This is a reaction to the time when there was a great overemphasis on God as a stern judge, a person more ready to condemn than to forgive. Spiritual life for many was based more on fear of hell than on love of God. We do not want to return to that.

The emphasis today on God's mercy and love is certainly a good thing, but we must not let it lull us into an unrealistic feeling that anything we do is OK because God is standing by with his first-aid kit. From some preachers we almost get the impression that God is emotionally crushed if we don't sin enough for him to exercise his mercy.

On second thought, there is no need to talk of God's mercy if we are unaware of sin in the first place.

There is also much discussion today of the sinful condition in which we find ourselves, of our estrangement from God, and the reconciliation which must be made. When we are born we cannot be held responsible for this condition, which we call original sin, but this does not excuse us from responsibility for individual sins.

Again, our life must be seen as a whole, but a whole is made up of parts. Our life is a succession of decisions and actions. Jesus, who is our moral guide, does not merely talk of the human condition. Time and time again he lists specifics—you fed me or did not feed me, you gave me a drink or did not give me a drink, you clothed me or did not clothe me, you welcomed me, a stranger, or you did not welcome me, you comforted me in my illness or you did not, you visited me in prison or you did not.

IT'S NOT ALL PSYCHOLOGY

Over and over Jesus tells us what to do and what not to do. And he also tells us that we will be judged for eternity on what we have done and on what we have failed to do. In telling us that we will be judged he is telling us that God holds us responsible for our actions. That day, inevitably, is coming for each one of us. We can try to hide, as did Adam and Eve in the creation story, but there will be no place to hide.

John Leonard, the TV reviewer for the *New York Times,* wrote recently: "We seem to have settled for blaming evil on psychopathology or childhood trauma, preferably a combination of both. . . . Something is missing—and has been for a long time. That something is a sense of sin. . . . A sense of sin seems almost to have become nothing more than a literary idea, belonging in the classroom where Blake and Dostoyevsky are taught."

Much earlier, Pope Pius XII had said that the ultimate sin is to say that there is no sin.

Sin is an evil human act. The Mass begins with a confession of sins. We should take that confession seriously, not just routinely rattle off the words. We can ask ourselves, "When did I last say and really mean, 'I am guilty of committing a sin?' "

"See what love the Father has bestowed on us," writes St.

John, "in letting us be called children of God! Yet that is what we are. . . . Everyone who sins acts lawlessly for sin is lawlessness. You know well that the reason he revealed himself was to take away sin" (1 John 3:1, 4, 5).

We may not intend it to be so, but each sin is a refusal of God's love.

The Ten Commandments Aren't Enough

The disease that felled so many people at the Bellevue Hotel in Philadelphia during a convention of the American Legion is now called Legionnaires' Disease. When it crops up in various places the news media simply term it the Legionnaires' Disease. I imagine that the American Legion does not like that designation. But we like simplistic terms.

So do the Legionnaires. Some years ago, in an effort to improve the moral tone of the country, they furnished large framed copies of the Ten Commandments to schools and other public buildings. I guess the idea was that if we all just obeyed the Ten Commandments the country would be OK. The American Legion did not do much research on the origin and background of the Decalogue (the commandments were called the ten words, or principles).

Neither have most people. When I mentioned to someone after Mass one Sunday that I had been asked to write a book on sin she said, "Just give them the Ten Commandments, Father." I did not have time then to explain to her what a simplistic and ineffective solution that was.

Life would be easier, perhaps, if we had a simple rule book to follow. Just check off ten simple rules each day and then pull out a plum and say "what a good boy am I." But life is more complicated than that. When the Ten Commandments were first written down, no one knows when (and hardly by Moses), they were intended for a people relatively small in number struggling to become a nation.

The Decalogue was a covenant law formulated to facilitate life in the community; at the time, no universal application was expected. The commandments were laws for the Hebrews, not for other people (though some laws were similar to laws of pagan neighbors). Many, many other laws were promulgated for Jews in Old Testament times. Thus it was that Christ could be asked, "Teacher, which commandment of the law is the greatest?" (Mt. 23:36).

In answer Christ did not give any of the Ten Commandments, but he quoted the Book of Deuteronomy (6:5) about loving God with one's whole heart, soul, and strength. In ancient times, though, that god was a national god, a god only of the chosen race, not a god of all people. And when Christ quoted the second law, love of neighbor, to the Hebrews *neighbor* meant a fellow countryman, a member of the Hebrew community, not just anybody (Leviticus 19:18).

Centuries later, Christ taught that his Father was the God of everyone and that our neighbor included everyone in the world, even our enemies. But the times of the Ten Commandments did not see it that way. The spiritual growth of any people, of course, takes a long time to develop. There are even two sets of Ten Commandments in the Old Testament, the first in Exodus (20:1-17) and the second representing a later development in Deuteronomy (5:6-21).

ONE MOST HIGH GOD

Catholics, Jews, and Protestants, though agreeing on the Ten Commandments, number them differently. Probably what we consider only the first commandment should be divided into two commandments, and the last two made one. The *two* tablets may have referred to two copies, such as are made for the two parties of a covenant.

"I, the Lord, am your God, who brought you out of the land of slavery," begin the commandments. In early times people believed in many gods. Each nation and each family wanted its own gods. The Hebrews were to have their own in Yahweh. The Hebrews may have accepted the existence of other gods, but Yahweh was exclusively their own. Gods were limited to their own turf. When Solomon married many foreign princesses each brought her own gods. Jezebel, likewise, brought her gods when she married Ahab. Thus was violated the command, "You shall have no other gods besides me."

But the Hebrew God, though jealous, is not to be put in one's pocket; he is not a possession; he is not to be controlled. Thus there are to be no human-made images of him to be carried around at the will of the owner. He is totally the other, transcendent, free, who reveals himself in the history of humanity where and when he wills. Later he will be revealed in Jesus Christ. But even today we violate the spirit of this commandment when we try to get too cozy with God, especially in our liturgy.

Reverence for God's name is reverence for God himself. The name stood for the person. God was not to be controlled or used or made a weapon by using his name and therefore using him. In ancient times the name of god was used in magic and sorcery, in rituals and incantations. The god, in a sense, was forced to respond. In Hebrew the words *in vain* literally mean "for unreality." God's name cannot be used in an empty or insincere or frivolous manner. God was not to be subject to the will or activity of the Israelites.

LABOR LAW

The command to abstain from work on the Sabbath was a merciful law. There were no labor unions then to prevent an employer from overworking his slaves. This longest of the commandments, in its full text, points out that Israel is a religious nation. The law, though, is more a social and humanitarian legislation than primarily a religious one. Nothing is said about worship or religious services.

"To put it very plainly and very definitely," writes William Barclay, Scripture professor, "this third commandment is not binding on the Christian at all, for there is no evidence in Scripture that the rules and regulations which govern the Sabbath were ever transferred by divine authority to the Lord's Day."

Interpreters of the fourth commandment usually err in making this a commandment for children only. The commandment orders us to *honor* our parents; it does not say *obey* them. Obedience may be part of honor, but honor is a more far-reaching term. The commandment applied especially to adults. In primitive societies old people became economically useless. There could be the temptation to turn the aged parents out to starve.

Israel was a patriarchal society. It was not a case of mommy, daddy, and kiddies. We might notice that low as the status of woman was in Hebrew society this commandment mentions the mother. Sons were not to banish or cause the death of parents by non support—something we might remember today when we consider the nursing-home scandals in some cities.

In an age which idiotically worships youth the fourth commandment should be brought to the fore. Reverence for old age has unhealthily been forgotten. A person's value and human dignity comes not from economic worth but from one's status as a child of God.

"You shall not kill" did not forbid all killing. The ancient Hebrews killed men, women, and children as they fought their way into the promised land. "You shall not murder" would be a better translation (though English does not have an exact word for the Hebrew); it refers especially to the murder of another Hebrew.

The sixth commandment, which in so much of the church's pastoral direction and moral teaching wrongly reigned over all the others, actually had to do more with justice than with sex. It did not forbid a Jew from having sexual intercourse with a prostitute or a woman taken captive in war. The wife was the possession of the husband and it was wrong for someone else to use his property. Purity or chastity were not at stake here, but Jewish society needed a stable married life. Polygamy was legal, and divorce was not only allowed (by the husband), it was sometimes mandatory by law.

"You shall not steal" is more difficult to interpret. It is generally thought that it forbade kidnapping a free Israelite man, usually for the purpose of making him a slave or selling him (as Joseph's brothers did to him).

"You shall not bear false witness against your neighbor" was not a commandment not to lie. There were other prohibitions to lying. It meant simply what it says. The administration of law was the responsibility of elders or local leaders; there was not the complex court mechanism we have now. A decision was made on the testimony of two witnesses. Women were not allowed to give witness. The sentence was immediate. Thus we see how necessary it was for a regulated community life that a witness not lie or even be devious in his testimony or even give irrelevant testimony.

In order to get Naboth's vineyard for her husband King Ahab, Jezebel got two scoundrels to testify that Naboth had cursed God and king. "And they (the elders) led him out of the city and stoned him to death." She then told Ahab to take possession of the land, for Naboth was dead (1 Kings 21:1-16).

THE TEN COMMANDMENTS NOT ENOUGH

Women will not be flattered that they are listed along with the neighbor's ass as things not to be coveted in the ninth and tenth commandments. The earlier version lists first the house (tent), then the wife and other possessions. The later version lists the wife first and makes a change in the verb for the other things. One must not *covet* the wife and not *set one's heart* on the other property.

To covet does not merely mean to desire; when we stop desiring we are dead. To the Semitic mind *covet* included all the planning and intrigue to usurp another's property. To covet is to make the necessary moves to get something unjustly. We are familiar with the story of the fall of Jericho; the walls came tumbling down when the priests blew their horns as loud as a rock band and the people shouted. The Israelites then rushed in and put to the sword "all living creatures in the city: men and women, young and old."

But in attacking the next city the Israelites lost because Achan kept treasure for himself in the Jericho loot, treasure reserved for the temple. "In my greed I coveted them (a mantle, gold and silver bars) and took them," admits Achan. He and his family are then stoned to death (Joshua 6-7).

The Ten Commandments were guides for another time,

17

place, and society. But they do teach that God cares, and they do teach reverence for God and respect for our neighbor. They are a primitive effort to help people live in community. They are the opening to a bill of rights for humanity.

We cannot simply memorize them or rattle them off and then think that we have a complete moral guide for today. Christ came to reveal more fully the one God of eternity. We must hear God in our time.

Cheating Hearts

THEFT, FRAUD, CORRUPTION. . . . That's the headline of the daily newspaper I am reading at the moment. "So what else is new?" I want to say. For theft, fraud, and corruption are hardly news. Yet the words in the headline are three inches high. It is no use. We are not shocked anymore by theft, fraud, and corruption, even if they are reported in huge letters.

The story under the headlines tells of corruption in the motor vehicle registration office of one state. The employees, "public servants," had stolen millions of dollars of license fees. I decided to go through the rest of the newspaper and make two lists, one of bad news and one of good news. You guessed it, the bad news won—by a landslide. In fact there were only two pieces of good news.

One item of good news was that 50,000 whistles were to be distributed at a series of crime-prevention clinics for old people. This was happening, of course, because of the bad news that old people increasingly are being attacked and robbed. The other piece of good news was that New York City would be able to borrow some money at 6.3 percent interest. This followed the bad news that the city was nearly broke.

The rest of the paper was bad news—a city clerk steals $2500 in the Parking Violations Bureau, a weatherman is fired from his TV job, a cop's mother is slain, a man loots an apartment after a fire, a mother with a 14-year-old lover lets her eight children starve, an indignant mom sues the Board of Education, a man is robbed and shot, terror grips a neighborhood, a husband and wife fleece thousands of people in a get-rich-quick scheme, an orchestra is going on strike, five people are found guilty of defrauding the school lunch program, etc., etc., etc.

The sports pages came out even—for the winners it was good news, for the losers it was bad news.

We live in such a milieu of bad news, it seems. And the bad news found in that day's edition of the paper was not natural bad news such as floods or drought, but moral bad news. It was news of sin. We seem to be surrounded by evil.

The tragic thing is that our young people are aware of the pervasive evil. And it is sad that some do not see it as evil, but only as a way of life, a means of survival. For example, robbery and beating of old and crippled people by young people aged 11 to 14 is on the increase at a fast rate. Recently a boy of 11 cooly and calmly told on TV how he and other kids his age planned their robberies and beatings of old people. They even staked out territories. There was not the slightest remorse or sense of wrongdoing in his attitude.

To him, doing evil was a good way of life. He had learned well from his elders. Monkey see, monkey do. But not only young people are inclined to do what others are doing; we also are tempted by the morals of this world—the world over which, Christ said, the devil is prince.

NO ONE IS EXEMPT

Partly it is because we get discouraged about doing good. We feel we are the fall guy, that others are making suckers out of us. We see what other people seem to be getting by with, and we get cynical. "I may as well get my slice of the pie too," we reason.

"Everybody's doing it," becomes our justification. And it is true that we are born into a sinful world. At birth we are not isolated from sinful humanity, we are part of it. "Each of us," as one writer puts it, "contributes to the sin condition of the race. For good or ill we affect those who come after us."

J.A.T. Robinson, in commenting on the book of *Genesis,* says that "sin is something that may not be understood in terms of one generation alone." No one person or age is wholly responsible for the sin in the world. "All men, he writes, "find themselves born into an historical order where sin is there before them, dragging them down. Go back into history as far as one may, one can find no generation and no civilization in which this is not true. There seems to be no time when sin was not there anticipating individual choice and decision."

A.M. Dubarle in *The Biblical Doctrine of Original Sin* comes to much the same conclusion. "We see original sin," he writes, "as a truly tragic and actual situation ... the moral and religious perversion in which every man finds himself inevitably plunged by reason of his birth into a perverted environment: ignorance of God, or idolatry and a more or less profound corruption."

"Mankind is oppressed by a countless mass of sins," declares Dubarle, "it is impossible accurately to pinpoint the individual responsibility for this. In each generation the harmfulness of this distant downfall is reactivated by new sins. And the pressure of the social environment forces some of this corruption into the empty souls of children, just as physical heredity transmits blemishes or some lack of balance. Nobody can claim to have escaped this condition: everyone needs a Savior."

We can admit all this, call it original sin or whatever, yet we must not despair before such conditions, or give up, or excuse our participation in evil. God saw the evil in the world but he did not give up or he would not have sent his Son. If God has confidence in our chances of being holy and not evil then we also ought to have confidence in ourselves—or at least have confidence in God.

SLIPPING INTO SIN

I think that it is in small ways that we begin to join the forces of evil. We begin to cheat; we begin to take advantage of other people. We each have our small, secret, slimy ways of cheating. Cheating defrauds another person of something, and it is done deceptively. Because it is done quietly and secretly we are the more easily tempted to do it. And we say we owe it to ourselves, that we are just getting what we really deserve because we have been cheated or defrauded of our goods or been gypped or even robbed.

Cheating is a thing that "nice" people can do. It is a silent way of slipping into sin, nothing public about it. As Samuel Johnson wrote, "Most vices may be committed very genteelly; a man may cheat at cards genteelly."

When the Savior did come and John the Baptizer preached his advent, people asked, "What ought we to do?" John's piety was very practical. He told the tax collectors, in effect, not to cheat. He told the soldiers to be content with their pay, and he told the other people to give one coat away, if they had two, and to share their food. We can't be covetous and have Christ at the same time.

John's bluntness must have been hard to take. If only he had used some roundabout language or mere generalizations. If only he had been more vague and inexact. Why did he insist on giving examples? "Exact nothing over and above your fixed amounts." That was said to the tax collectors, but it is said to us also.

"Let the man who has two coats give to him who has none. The man with food should do the same." Wham! What are we going to do with that? John could not be more direct. But there it is. Many of us are figuring out how to get a third coat, or a fourth or fifth coat. How many pounds of food go into the garbage pail in one week in our home? Are we genteelly cheating others of food and clothing and other necessities?

CHEATING OURSELVES

We do not mention these things in order to reproach anyone. Only to point out that when we think we are being cheated by the world—which, it must be admitted, is cheating us of material goods every chance it gets—and we get covetous and want to cheat back, we are really cheating ourselves of something far more important and valuable—we are cheating ourselves of Christ.

We are cheating ourselves of "God's own peace, which is beyond all understanding" (Phil. 4:7). We are like the three thieves who before dividing their loot decided to have something to eat. One went out to get the food. While he was gone the other two planned to kill him on his return and keep his share for themselves. But he, meanwhile, decided to kill them and take their share. So he poisoned the food. You guessed it—on his return the other two jumped him and killed him. And then they unknowingly ate the poisoned food and died.

About 95 percent of us, I suspect, feel that we are underpaid. One of the people found guilty of cheating poor children of food in the government lunch program was making a salary of $26,000 a year. We can always find a reason for cheating, one that slips by our conscience quite easily. Or not notice when we in effect are cheating others of the goods they need. "Feed the man dying of hunger," declared Vatican Council II, "because if you have not fed him you have killed him."

Missioners have seen children die because families did not possess the equivalent of 25 cents to buy worm medicine to save them. "Every gun that is made, every warship that is launched, every rocket fired signifies, in the final sense," said President Eisenhower, "a theft from those who hunger and are not fed, those who are cold and are not clothed."

When we are tempted to cheat, and it is always at someone else's expense, we should remember Christ's warning: "You fool! This very night your life shall be required of you. To whom will all this piled-up wealth of yours go?" (Luke 12:20). Means of cheating are usually subtle, and there are many ways. And many things of which people can be cheated. We could make a good examination of conscience just by asking ourselves, "How often did I cheat today?"

I see employers cheating their workers and I see employees cheating their employers, and businessmen cheating their customers. And I see parents cheating their children of the discipline and guidance they need. And on it goes.

But a Christian with trust in God must refuse absolutely to cheat in any way. "If God clothes in such splendor the grass of the field, which grows today and is thrown on the fire tomorrow," Christ tells us, "how much more will he provide for you, O weak in faith! ... The unbelievers of this world are always running after such things. ... Seek out instead his kingship over you, and the rest will follow" (Luke 12:28, 30, 31).

Greed
Shows

It is said that in former times when a new pope received the triple crown, the tiara, amidst all the splendor and pomp of a papal coronation in the magnificent basilica of St. Peter's, an official would stand before him and blow a light feather off his hand saying, *Sic transit gloria mundi,* thus passes the glory of the world.

This old Latin expression is a good warning not only to popes not to be seduced by the power and glory of the papacy, but also is a good warning to anyone who gets too involved with the affairs of this world, too intent on amassing material goods for himself or for achieving financial or social power.

"Everything is vanity" is the theme of the Old Testament book of Ecclesiastes. The word vanity comes from the Hebrew word for breath or vapor. It is used 35 times in Ecclesiastes, so strongly does the author wish to emphasize that our life on earth may vanish at any moment, that life is as short and light as a breath.

In this matter Christ is as blunt and direct as ever: "Avoid greed in all its forms . . . possessions do not guarantee life . . . you fool, this very night your life shall be required of you." Christ was not talking to bank presidents at a Rotary banquet; he was talking to the ordinary people who crowded around him, talking to people who owned very little.

Such texts as *sic transit gloria mundi* or *you fool, this night* are good ones to paste on the bathroom mirror or some other place where we will see them every day. They would remind us that we are born anew, that we have put on the new man, and such texts would help keep our thoughts, ambitions, and desires on the things that are above (Col. 3:1-3).

Surely, we may enjoy the good things that God gives us in this life. We do not despise God's creation and we need not feel guilty about delighting in God's material gifts. But they can gradually begin to take over; we can get slowly more and more covetous of them; we can forget to see them objectively in the light of God's total plan for our salvation.

THINGS OR GOD?

We are more important to God than all these things, than all of the vast material universe; we must not let these things become more important to us than God our Father. That's why St. Paul tells us to set our hearts on what pertains to higher realms where Christ is seated at God's right hand. Christ, who is now with his Father, on earth had no place to lay his head, and the only thing he had left before his death, his seamless robe, was taken away.

Much as we may cherish earthly things for one reason or another, apart from absolute greed, it is pitiful to see anyone clutch too greedily to any earthly thing or be anxious for wealth. Hetty Green, for one example, was a New York multimillionaire who died in 1916. In her love for her money she ate at the cheapest restaurants and would haggle over the price of a pair of shoes. When she complained about paying ten cents for a bottle of medicine the druggist pointed out that the bottle itself cost five cents. So she went home to get her own bottle and paid five cents for the medicine.

When her son Ned hurt his knee she was too stingy to call a doctor, and treated it herself. Two years later it still had not healed, so, hoping for charity, she dressed him in rags to make believe that she was poor and took him to a doctor. When the doctor learned who she was he asked for payment. So she took her son away and never went back. Because she was too attached to her money to give her son the proper care, his leg had to be amputated. She had $100 million when she died.

No, none of us has that much money. But in small ways we

can have the same avaricious spirit. Such an outlook on life is really sad. We might take inventory, looking at each thing that we own, and see if we look at it under the aspect of eternity. How attached are we to it? Does possession of it, and the lust for more things, lead us into other sins? Covetousness or greed is one of the capital sins because it leads us into so many other sins.

It may seem strange to talk of greed when there is so much actual poverty in the world. But we will not get rid of the poverty until we get rid of the sin of greed in the hearts of all people. We must raise our sights to the things that are above and we must seek first the kingdom of God. And then, as Christ says, all the things needed here below will be taken care of by our heavenly Father (Mt. 6:33).

Trust in Divine Providence needs constant emphasis. We can talk our heads off about justice and peace in the world and about the elimination of destitution, but there will be injustice, strife, and inhuman poverty until we truly follow Christ, follow him in his spirit of poverty.

WALL OF GREED

When Jesus first called certain people to follow him he called them to be disciples. Other teachers of the law, especially Pharisees, also had groups of disciples. These disciples learned from a master and teacher they respected. But Christ demanded more from his disciples; he made rigorous demands on them. Among his requirements were that they leave money and wealth (Mark 10:21) and economic security (Luke 9:58). They were to learn not only by listening but by doing.

The evangelists later applied this notion of discipleship to all Christians. All were to take up their cross and follow Christ. This did not mean that all were to live in material poverty, but all were to remove whatever became a wall separating them from God. In the case of the rich young man his riches barred him from perfection. So Christ told him to sell what he had, give to the poor the results of the sale, and follow Christ. The man was too attached to his riches to give them up.

The man "went away sad"; for, though Christ promised

him riches in heaven, he preferred those of earth. Where your treasure is, Christ told us, there is your heart. Our greed keeps us from real treasure, everlasting happiness.

Greed is an unpleasant word, a distasteful word. It is not a popular word, and I think that we would rather confess to pride, the mother of all sins, rather than to confess to greed. Homilists generally avoid the word. In fact, they avoid the word *sin*. I have just read through dozens of sermons or homilies from companies offering homiletic services and found the word *sin* in only one homily.

I realize that this avoidance of the word is a reaction to the days when we had an obsession with lists of specific sins and that now there is an emphasis on our sinful condition or our alienation from God; but it seems to me that we will not be aware of our sinful condition unless we are aware of sins.

If a medical doctor told a patient, "You're sick," and then did not analyze the illness in specific terms and tell the patient what to do for a cure, the doctor would soon have no patients. The reality of sin is all around us and within us. We do not make it disappear by making believe that it does not exist. Greed, avarice, covetousness for material goods is one of the most pervasive of sins. It is responsible for so many other sins.

Just see how many news stories are accounts of greed. Again and again we find public officials guilty of it. Big business is finally being exposed by the news media. Only four percent of members of labor unions think their union leaders are of high moral character. Slum youngsters slice up helpless old women in order to get their Social Security money. Avarice is so ever-present that we might look into ourselves to see if it lurks there also.

Scripture does not hesitate to talk about it. In both the Old and the New Testament there are many, many references to it and warnings about it.

"He who is greedy of gain," says the book of Proverbs, "brings ruin on his own house" (16:27). "The covetous man is never satisfied with money," we read in Ecclesiastes, "and the lover of wealth reaps no fruit from it; so this too is vanity" (5:9).

John the Baptist was very practical about rooting out avarice. When asked by his listeners how they could make their lives more fruitful he told them to share their food and clothing with their neighbors. He demanded that the tax collectors exact nothing over and above the fixed amounts, and he told the soldiers to be content with their pay (Lk 3:10-14). Judas is a classic example of greed and what it can lead to. His greed led him to betray his friend into death (Mt. 26:14-16).

Paul warned that "those who want to be rich are falling into temptation and a trap; they are letting themselves be captured by foolish and harmful desires which drag men down to ruin and destruction" (1 Tim. 6:9). He himself told the presbyters at Miletus, "Never did I set my heart on anyone's silver or gold" (Acts 20:33). He believed Christ, who said, "You cannot give yourself to God and money" (Mt. 6:24).

Faith, love of God and neighbor, liberality, the virtues of hope and justice can prevent us from falling into the everlasting pit of which George Herbert (1593-1633) spoke when he wrote of money, mined as gold and silver from the ground:

> Man calleth thee his wealth, who made thee rich;
> And while he digs out thee, falls in the ditch.

I Could
Care Less

"Bless me, Father, for I have sinned. My last confession was a year ago. I beat up my wife twice, I stole nine dollars from the office petty cash fund, I missed Mass several Sundays, and I committed the sin of acedia three times. For these and any other sins I may have forgotten I am heartily sorry and beg absolution of you, Father."

It might just be worthwhile going back to confession and trying that on the confessor.

"That might be a good joke for April Fool's Day," you might answer me, "but basically it would be dishonest. I never beat up my wife (she's bigger than I am) and I never stole from the petty cash fund (too difficult to get at it). Though I do admit I missed Mass quite a few Sundays (just couldn't be bothered).

"But acedia, I certainly never committed that in my lifetime. That's for sure.

"As a matter of fact, I am spiritually too weary to commit that. I have too much spiritual torpor for that, too much ennui in the spiritual life. I have become too dejected, almost dead, in the presence of Divine Good to bother with the sin of acedia. It makes me even too melancholy to think about spiritual life, much less a violation of it. Really, I am indifferent. I could care less. By the way, just what is acedia?"

And I would answer, "Guilty, as charged. You have just described the sin of acedia, the seventh capital sin."

Sloth is usually listed as the last of the seven capital sins, but more properly speaking, it may be the result of acedia. The seven capital sins are sins from which other sins flow. One moral theology book describes sloth in the terms we use for acedia, "a tedium over the friendship of God because of the efforts necessary to maintain that friendship."

"This kind of sloth," the author adds, "is directly opposed to the love of God, and is, therefore, gravely sinful by its very nature."

Missing Mass on Sunday could be the result of acedia. Not bothering with the sacrament of reconciliation for a whole year, though not necessarily a sin in itself, also could be the result of acedia. The term comes from the Greek word for "not caring." Sometimes it is described as a sadness or a weariness opposed to the joy we should find in spiritual good. One early church Father refers to the Book of Quoheleth (Ecclesiastes) in the Old Testament, "All things are full of weariness, more than man can utter" (1:18).

Guerric, the second abbot of the Cistercian abbey of Igny (d. 1157) says, "Are not spiritual weariness and sadness a worm? Truly it is a vice which can slowly worm its way into ourselves." Guerric refers to the Book of Proverbs, "As the moth to a garment and as worm to wood, so does a man's sadness harm his heart."

AN ANCIENT, YET MODERN SIN

In the early days of the church this was a sin over which the desert monks were especially concerned. By the time of St. Gregory the Great, however, it was considered a sin which every Christian had to be aware of. And six daughter sins were listed: malice, rancor, pusillanimity, despair, torpor concerning the commandments, and a wandering of the mind around forbidden things.

For St. Thomas Aquinas acedia is opposed to the joy of charity. It directly attacks our joy in the divine good. Hence, it can be the cause of many other sins. The generic word *sloth* is usually used in listing the capital sins today, but acedia is a wider term and is a more serious sin than mere laziness. This apathy, this deadness of the soul, was considered an extremely serious sin.

It is a sin much in evidence today, a sin whose time has

come round again, a sin more subtle than others, and a sin which by its very nature makes us unaware of itself. We see it in the many who are leaving the church today; we see it in the lessened attendance at the sacraments, the casual air with which people miss Sunday Mass, the loss of vocations to the religious life, the decreased support of the church.

We see it in a weakened prayer life, in the loss of religious values, in the apathetic attitudes of people, in the loss of joy in the Lord. The recent and rather sudden rise in pentecostalism is probably a reaction to this acedia. Just as there was no joy in Mudville the day mighty Casey struck out, for many people today there seems to be no joy in the church—as though Jesus had struck out.

Again and again in the Gospels and Epistles and in the Acts of the Apostles we see the word and we sense the happiness and enthusiasm of the sacred authors. If there was reason for interest, for life, for joy, then there still is reason now, for God is as good as ever.

Satan, in the gospel story, asks Jesus, "What have I to do with you, O Jesus of Nazareth, holy one of God?" Will we align ourselves with Satan? But perhaps Satan at least has enthusiasm for evil. We are merely listless and have no taste for the spiritual life. Satan is in anguish before God; we are merely bored.

There is a sadness about this sin, and one can see why it is such a serious sin. Perhaps it is the ultimate sin; it even reduces the importance of the other sins. Truly, it is the most saddening of the sins. Perhaps it more than the other capital sins reduces a person's spirit to blah. The other six capital sins (pride, covetousness, lust, anger, gluttony, and envy) have some energy about them, even a perverse dignity of life, a zest for something. But acedia is closer to death, death of the human spirit.

THE CURE FOR ACEDIA

It is no wonder that even great saints, and especially the ascetical monks of the desert in the early centuries of the church, worried about this sin. St. Anthony the Great, called The Father of Monks, born in Egypt about 251 A.D., heard the gospel message of Christ, "Go sell all that you have and give to the poor and come, follow me." Henceforth he devoted himself to a life of asceticism. Although he went out into the desert as a recluse his wisdom and holiness attracted followers. He lived to be 105 years old.

Yet this great man was afflicted by the temptation to acedia. And he was wise enough and experienced enough to recognize the temptations for what they were. In *The Sayings of the Desert Fathers,* a centuries-old compendium of the wisdom and experiences of the desert Fathers, we read that Anthony was beset by acedia. "Lord," he prayed, "I want to be saved but these thoughts do not leave me alone; what shall I do in my affliction? How can I be saved?"

In a little while Anthony got up to go out, and then he saw a man like himself sitting at his work, getting up from work to pray, and then sitting down again at his work of plaiting rope, and then getting up again to pray. The man was an angel of the Lord sent to help him and to reassure him. The angel said, "Do this and you will be saved." These words filled Anthony with courage and joy, and he decided to follow the example of that man.

Indeed, *Ora et Labora* (Pray and Work) later became the motto of the Benedictine monks. Dom Germain Morin, in commenting on the Rule of St. Benedict, says, "The surest sign by which to judge the fervor of any community is the joy that they reflect." He calls acedia the bane of true joy.

Abba Poemen, a desert ascetic, when asked about the vice of acedia, replied, "Acedia is there every time one begins something, and there is no worse passion, but if a man recognizes it for what it is, he will gain peace."

GOOD AND BAD GRIEF

"There is grief that is useful, and there is grief that is destructive," advises Syncletica, a woman contemplative. "The first consists in weeping over one's own faults and weeping over the weakness of one's neighbors, in order not to destroy one's purpose, and attach oneself to the perfect good. But there is also a grief that comes from the enemy, full of mockery, which some call *acedia.* This spirit must be cast out, mainly by prayer and psalmody."

With a God and a life to be so excited about it is pitiful to see people beset by acedia, and especially to see some young people who take the stance of boredom with life, who want to be "cool," distant from everything, uninvolved, unengaged in the world God has given us to live and work in. When we are bored with God, our creator, we must turn to something less.

Cassian, who wrote his famous *Institutes of the Coenobia,* a treatise on the monastic life, devotes a whole book to the evil of acedia. The *Institutes* were written between 419 and 426 A.D., but their wisdom and advice, though written for monks, are most helpful for anyone developing a life of the Spirit in our times. "The true Christian athlete who desires to strive lawfully in the lists of perfection," writes Cassian, "should hasten to expel this disease also from the recesses of his soul."

Let us hope that the readers have not been driven to acedia, the last of the deadly sins, by having read thus far.

Everybody's Doing It

Two boys, late one evening, were standing in front of a store window. "Come on," said the one boy to the other. But the other did not move; he shook his head and said, "No."

"But everyone is doing it," rejoined the one. But the other still would not budge. His companion then jumped through the window; the large plate glass had already been smashed by looters.

The incident is true. It was the time of the blackout in New York City. The news media gave lurid and hyped-up accounts of the looting, as though the whole city had been looted. Actually it was only in certain neighborhoods. The excuse given by the looters, later interviewed by the press and TV, was that "everyone was doing it."

The conscience of the one boy simply would not let him go in and loot. He was safe—it was dark; there were no police around; mobs of people around him were looting. He had the opportunity—he could have grabbed some things and run home with them.

But he would also have to take his conscience home with him. His conscience may have told him that he had robbed a "ma and pa store," a small store run by two elderly people who depended on it for a living. Or he may have looted a store finally built up after long years by someone from an underprivileged minority. Or robbing the store may have meant its closing for good and a consequent loss of jobs in a poor neighborhood.

In his frenzy to loot, the other boy ripped his arm on broken plate glass and had to be taken to a hospital. He was partly correct, though, in saying "everyone's doing it." For there are many forms of looting—some hurried, sudden, and almost hysterical, as in the case of the blackout looting, and some genteel and carefully planned.

Just a few months ago a doctor spent half an hour operating on the little finger of a poor foreign student. She billed him $1045.00 for the operation. That was only for the operation, not for hospital or operating-room expenses. The operation was not a success, for the finger is now permanently crooked, is painful, and swells in warm weather. The doctor may have known that the patient would apply for medicaid, and thus the doctor would bilk the taxpayers for that outrageous sum.

Corporation heads loot the citizens by finding loopholes so taxes can be avoided. Daily there are news stories of government employees, from the highest paid to the lowest paid, who are looting the agencies they are working for. We can loot other people even emotionally.

All through history looting was concomitant with warfare. The ancient Hebrews, in the name of God, looted and pillaged their way into the promised land. They were not unusual in doing that, for it was a way of life for nations—get ahead by pillaging your neighbor. Cave men looted, and the practice continued right on into the Second World War, when American soldiers looted in Europe. Jungle tribes do it and powerful nations do it.

There are many ways of looting and we are all capable of it. Then, there we sit and look at our sad pile of loot and God says, "You fool, this very night your life shall be required of you" (Luke 12:20).

WHAT WOULD JESUS DO?

Whenever we are tempted to loot or to sin in any way we must ask, "Is Jesus asking me to do this?" We are not to ask, "Is it safe? Is anyone watching? Can I get away with it? Will anyone find out? Will I be punished?" We can only ask the fundamental question, "Is this what Jesus calls me to do?"

In one of our largest cities 950 government employees were accused of bilking the welfare system. In other areas grand juries indicted 337 public figures in one year. I imagine that each culprit had an excuse. For excuses come handily when we want to loot: Everybody's doing it. It's a form of protest against the system; I want to get my share of the pie; if I don't grab it someone else will. It's today's way of life. They're cheating us by their prices. The list is endless and can be much more ingenious.

But none of the excuses are provided for us by Jesus.

"Talk is cheap," my housekeeper once blurted out, "but it takes money to buy whiskey." She was a little embarrassed at having said it, but it was a bit of practical wisdom she had heard from a farmhand. And it is true; we can make excuses for our sins and we can pray "Lord, Lord," but our heavenly Father sees our motives, sees us making those painful, lonely moral decisions. Mere talk will not get us salvation.

WE ARE RESPONSIBLE

No one else can make decisions for us and we cannot blame others for our decisions. Two boys stood in front of a shattered plate-glass window; each had to make his own decision. A corporation executive sits behind his broad desk deciding whether to manufacture an immoral means of warfare. A store clerk sees the opportunity of dropping some merchandise into her handbag. A man is figuring out his claims against an insurance company. Again and again we must decide to loot or not to loot.

Charles Dickens in *Great Expectations* gives us an example of excuses we can use when we make decisions violating our conscience. Pip, who had been brought up in the rude home of a blacksmith and who is now living away in a "higher class" home, happens to be in the locality of his childhood home. Loyalty and devotion to the people who raised him urge him to visit them and stay with them overnight.

Yet his pride makes him ashamed to return to the simple cottage, and he "began to invent reasons and make excuses for putting up at the Blue Boar" (an inn) rather than staying in the blacksmith's humble abode.

After inventing excuses he admits to himself: "All other swindlers upon earth are nothing to the self-swindlers, and with such pretences did I cheat myself. Surely a curious thing. That I should innocently take a bad half-crown of somebody else's manufacture is reasonable enough; but that I should knowingly reckon the spurious coin of my own make as good money! An obliging stranger, under pretence of compactly folding up my bank notes for security's sake, abstracts the notes and gives me nutshells; but what is his sleight of hand to mine, when I fold up my own nutshells and pass them on myself as notes!"

Purity of intention is a difficult thing to achieve. There are so many opportunities to cheat, embezzle, steal, defraud, poach, swindle, fleece, and loot. We will not do these things if we realize that we have "been raised up in company with Christ," if we set our hearts "on what pertains to higher realms where Christ is seated at God's right hand," if we are "intent on things above rather than on things of earth" (Col. 3:1-2).

Do we want to grow rich for ourselves instead of growing rich in the sight of God (Luke 12:21)?

There is no time in which we can forget about Jesus. He must always be there to monitor our conscience. We must always be aware of his presence. We need him in every decision we make. Every time we are about to do something we must call him to our side. We must be able, without shame, to tell him what we are about to do.

What we are about to do must be something that Jesus himself would not object to doing. If we find that he could not do it then we simply must not do it. Christ is the guide to our conscience. If we are habitually aware of his presence it can prevent us from doing wrong on the spur of the moment. It will prevent a sudden blackout of the soul.

I am amazed at how casual some people are about their spiritual lives. Others think that they can jump up and down, wave their arms, scream "Jesus is Lord," and then think themselves saved. For them an analysis for the health of one's spiritual life is not to be thought of.

An examination of conscience is part of one's preparation for the sacrament of Penance or Rite of Reconciliation. With few people making use of this sacrament there may be few people making an examination of conscience. There is a brief time at the beginning of Mass for an examination, and we hope that the time is used for that. I realize that in the past the examination of conscience for confession sometimes was very superficial, but at least it was something.

There was also the danger for a few of becoming self-obsessed and scrupulous. But scrupulosity is rare today, and self-examination is still a healthful thing.

Elizabeth Ellion in *These Strange Ashes* tells a story of Jesus and his disciples. One day, so the account goes, Jesus and his disciples were walking along a stony road. Jesus asked each of them to choose a stone to carry for him. John, it is said, chose a large one while Peter chose the smallest.

Jesus led them then to the top of a mountain and commanded that the stones be made bread. Each disciple, by this time tired and hungry, was allowed to eat the bread he held in his hand. Peter's, of course, was not sufficient to satisfy his hunger. John gave him some of his.

Some time later Jesus again asked the disciples to pick up a stone to carry. This time Peter chose the largest of all. Taking them to a river, Jesus told them to cast the stones into the water. They did so, but looked at one another in bewilderment.

"For whom," asked Jesus, "did you carry the stone?"

To do as Jesus tells us must be our ultimate moral guide. "Your life is hidden now with Christ in God," says St. Paul. "What you have done is put aside your old self with its past deeds and put on a new man, one who grows in knowledge as he is formed anew in the image of his Creator.... Christ is everything in all of you" (Col. 3:3, 9-10).

"You can tell a tree by its fruit," Christ tells us. "None of those who cry out 'Lord, Lord' will enter the kingdom of God but only the one who does the will of my Father in heaven" (Mt. 7:21).

Which was Christ's way of saying, "Talk is cheap, but it takes money to buy whiskey."

Cast The First Stone?

King Frederick II of Prussia, so the story goes, once went to the prison at Spandau (where Rudolph Hess is today the solitary prisoner) to visit the prisoners. He asked each inmate why he was undergoing punishment, what crime the person had committed. One after another each person declared himself innocent of the crime of which he was convicted.

There was one exception, however. That person said, "I did a great wrong, your Majesty. The punishment I am undergoing is not half what I deserve."

"Then you have no business here among all these innocent persons," replied the king. "You may leave the prison." Thus the man was set free.

I sometimes wonder if that isn't the situation today among Catholics, if the tremendous drop-off in numbers of people participating in the sacrament of Penance or Rite of Reconciliation is due to the presumption of innocence of sin.

I realize that in the past we had too many classifications of sins, that we divided sin into multiple and minute categories, that we made too many fine moral distinctions, enough to make a person scrupulous or to leave one in confusion and fear.

Also, in sermons and in spiritual direction there was too great an emphasis on fear of hell, on God's wrath, on the immensity of punishment for even small sins, and a consequent lack of appreciation for the mercy and love of God. In some ways we were taught to despise ourselves.

For whatever reason, this teaching lost its hold on Catholics. It seems as though they would not accept it any longer. And at the same time preachers, spiritual directors, and theologians began to place strong and proper emphasis on God's love for us and on God's forgiving nature. This is certainly a healthful and good thing, for it is reality.

We again saw God not as a vengeful being ready to torture us for the least infraction of his law, but as a loving Father concerned about our eternal welfare. We saw him again as the good shepherd. And, concomitantly, we saw ourselves no longer as the bad guys but as the good guys. The danger, however, is that we listed ourselves among the 99 just.

A SINLESS PEOPLE?

Hence we feel no need for the sacrament of Penance. If we had nothing to confess there was no need to go to confession. Since God is so loving and merciful everything was taken care of. There was no need of absolution for nonexistent sins. I'm OK. Moral theology became an unpopular subject in schools and seminaries. Guilt feeling became a thing of the past. Anything we did which might be considered objectively wrong was the result of heredity, our genes, environment, or psychological necessity. I sometimes think that if Christ today said, "Let he who is without sin be the first to cast a stone," many people would look around for a stone to throw rather than silently slip away as did the group who brought to Christ the woman caught in adultery.

Yet some people still come to the confessional. And I am glad of that. I hope their number increases. For I know that there is something holy about persons who before God and others humbly admit their sins and ask forgiveness.

I am always impressed by each person who comes into the confessional or the reconciliation room who has the humility and the penitential spirit to accept responsibility for sins, and makes the effort to confess them, seeks pardon, and sincerely intends to overcome them.

I admire such people. And I must remark that it gives me a good feeling when I see such humility. Then I know that there is a good chance for growth in the spiritual life of the person. Even when I sense that the confession could be more complete or more sensitive to possible sins of omission I feel encouraged in the priestly work of the confessional. An imperfect confession is better than none at all.

A specific naming of sins is more difficult but also more beneficial than a general and vague confession such as we have in the confiteor at the beginning of Mass or at a penance service. This is not to say that we should not have acts of penitence at the beginning of the Mass or have public penance services, for both are good and useful; but if we do no more than that we could let our consciences fall asleep.

A HUMBLE AND CONTRITE HEART

It takes very little humility to recite in common an act of contrition, but it takes great humility to honestly admit and confess one's real sins. There is more emphasis today, I realize, on a person's sinful condition than on specific acts of sin, but we cannot cure the condition without finding the specific illnesses or wounds.

"The sacrament of Penance," says the introduction to the new rite of Penance, "includes the confession of sins, which comes from true knowledge of self before God and from contrition for those sins." Confession is good not only for those in grave sin. "Frequent and careful celebration of this sacrament," adds the introduction, "is also very useful as a remedy for venial sins. This is not a mere ritual repetition or psychological exercise, but a serious striving to perfect the grace of Baptism so that as we bear in our body the death of Jesus Christ, his life may be seen in us ever more clearly."

We hope that in both general and private confessions penitents make an honest and careful examination of conscience and are truly sorry for their sins. Some penitents making private confessions still seem to repeat the same sins, but to be regular is not necessarily routine, and even a routine confession is better than none at all.

Many predict that general confession will be the norm for the future, and many people prefer that to the private confession, but the numbers at general confession or penance services are not staggering. Most Catholics, it seems to me, are not taking part in the sacrament at all. Lack of growth in the Spirit will result from neglect of the sacrament.

Unless we frequently admit our sins and are truly sorry for them we could get into the habit of thinking that we have no sins. If we have no sins then Christ's mission on earth was foolishness. It is true that the lesser sins can be remitted by the reception of the Holy Eucharist, but that is not the primary end of the Eucharist.

HEALING THE WOUNDS OF SIN

Even venial sin, writes theologian Karl Rahner, "is an obstruction to the love of God and as such it is also an obstacle to the free and radiant development in this member of the church of that love which is poured out by the divine Spirit."

"Thus even venial sin is a spiritual injury," he adds, "an injustice to the whole Body of Christ. This Body, however, is visible; it is a historical magnitude. Hence, if the injustice done is to be repaired, then this could not happen more meaningfully and impressively than by acknowledging the sin before the priest, who is the representative of the community of Christ-believers, by having it forgiven by him, and atoning for it by the penance imposed, in order to make reparation for the injury done to the Body of Christ. To this extent, confession of devotion is not merely a continued practice of the love of God but also a unique form of sacramental love of neighbor."

The emphasis in this sacrament, of course, must be not so much on our confession as on the merciful love of God. The parable of the prodigal son is often given as an example of God's readiness to forgive. But we must not forget that the son first admitted his sins.

In the early centuries of the church, it is true, private confession, as far as we can ascertain, was almost nonexistent, and public confession was reserved for the most serious and public crimes or for one's deathbed. But this changed during the developing life of the church.

"If we say, 'We are free of the guilt of sin,' " says St. John, "we deceive ourselves; the truth is not to be found in us. But if we acknowledge our sins, he who is just can be trusted to forgive our sins and cleanse us from every wrong" (1 John 1:8-9).

In the Book of Numbers we read that the Lord told Moses

to tell the Israelites, "If men or women commit faults against their neighbors and wrong them, thus breaking faith with the Lord, they shall confess the wrong they have done, restore their ill-gotten goods in full, and in addition give one fifth of their value to the one they have wronged" (5:5-7).

Even one of the criminals hanging on the cross next to Jesus admitted his sins. "We are only paying the price for what we have done," he told the other criminal, "but this man has done nothing wrong." With Christ, it is true—he had done nothing wrong. We seem to put ourselves in the same category if we neglect the sacrament of Penance.

In a survey made by one diocesan paper a respondent thought that the young were taking God's mercy for granted. That may be. Presuming on God's mercy without admission of guilt and without true sorrow is presumption. In the parable of the publican and the pharisee we see that those who believe in their own self-righteousness are not likely to be saved.

Whether it is to the dark, stark, old confessional box or to the lamplit, carpeted, homey reconciliation parlor, we must make our way to it frequently for cleansing and healing, for humble acceptance of God's mercy.

There Is
A Better You!

"Did I ever tell you what happened to me in the confessional?" As soon as you begin telling someone the gory details of your surgical operation that person is sure to be reminded of his own operation and will want to tell you about it. The same thing happens if you tell a confessional story, an account of what happened to you on one occasion when you "went" to confession.

Often the experience was embarrassing, and the penitent is able to tell of it only years after its occurrence. With the decline in the number of private confessions today and a better understanding of the nature of the sacrament there will be fewer of those stories to tell. Perhaps someone should collect and publish an anthology of confessional stories, a genre of church stories which may pass out of existence. The anthology should open with Frank O'Connor's "My First Confession," one of the funniest stories I have ever read.

I thought of this again today after a friend recounted one of her confessional experiences. "I should have known better," she said. She was referring to the mistake she made in going to the confessional which had no line of penitents before it. Catholics learned by experience which confessors to avoid. If you came into a church for confession and there were lines of penitents near three confessionals but few or none at the fourth you knew the fourth was a confessional to avoid.

You suspected that the priest in the fourth confessional was too grouchy, or asked too many questions, or reexamined your conscience, or was partly deaf and therefore talked too loud. Though I did know one popular deaf confessor. Many people went to him because he could not hear them, yet he only whispered. You could go in and confess the most awful crimes, and he only quietly gave you three Hail Marys for a penance and then absolved you. "I just chopped my mother's head off and burned down the orphanage." "All right, for your penance say three Hail Marys. *Ego te absolvo....*"

My friend, however, happened to go to a confessional devoid of penitents because the priest was mostly deaf yet wanted to hear the whole confession. She confessed that she had missed Mass on Sunday because of psychological reasons. She told the priest that she had difficulty being close to other people—in churches, in crowded stores, in trains. All the confessor heard was the word *train.* So he shouted at her, with everyone else in the church as audience, *"What did you do on the train?"*

"I'm never going to leave this confessional," she thought in agony. "Everyone in the church will be looking at me."

Every Catholic accustomed to private confession in the stricter times before Vatican II would probably have their own horror story, now bitter or funny, to add to a compilation of confessional stories.

SPIRITUAL GUIDANCE

The charge is made, and it was often true, that going to confession became routine, that only surface sins, not real sins, were confessed, and that there was little spiritual improvement. Every confessor knows that this was not always the case. Many confessions came from deep in the heart and were real cries of repentance and an appeal for forgiveness and help. Many people were looking for spiritual guidance. In the new Rite of Reconciliation, with more time and more privacy, it will be easier to give this guidance than it was when penitents knelt briefly in the dark and had to whisper so people near the confessional and the penitent on the other side of the priest could not hear what was being confessed.

With the new Rite of Reconciliation there should be an increase in personal spiritual direction. We hope that priests will not try to become amateur psychologists, but that they will become more proficient in giving spiritual guidance.

People who make use of the new Rite of Reconciliation must, of course, see it as a means of repentance, sorrow, forgiveness, and reconciliation, and not primarily as an occasion for spiritual direction. Also, time could become a problem when there are a number of penitents. But the new rite should get people thinking again about personal spiritual direction.

Christ said, "You must be made perfect as your heavenly Father is perfect" (Mt. 5:48). How do we go about being made perfect? We plan most events in our lives. We plan our meals, our jobs, our schooling, our travels, parties, almost everything. But do we do any planning for that most important thing, our perfection?

The loss of faith, so prevalent today, cannot be blamed on liturgical changes or on developing doctrine. If we wander around aimlessly it is no wonder that we get lost. There is a school of thought today which tells us to accept ourselves as we are, the I'm OK thing. And that is good to a certain extent. There are certain given things in our race, our personality, our total makeup which we must accept. But we are creatures of free will and intellect, people who must be responsible for ourselves; we are not mere vegetables.

The prophets, the lawgivers, the evangelists, the authors of both the Old and the New Testament, and Jesus Christ, in their teachings presume that we are people capable of further perfecting ourselves, or, more properly, of allowing God to perfect us, through God's grace and help. Christ does not ask us to do what cannot be done.

GROWTH IN HOLINESS

In the Old Testament we find that the Lord said to Moses, "Speak to the whole Israelite community and tell them: Be holy, for I, the Lord, your God, am holy" (Lev. 19:2). Christ in the parable of the good seed falling on good ground lets us know that we can grow in holiness. Paul, too, says, "Let us profess the truth in love and grow to the full maturity of Christ" (Eph. 4:15).

In fact, the letter to the Ephesians might be a good guide

for beginning a probe into our spiritual growth, for planning a program of moving to perfection, "till we form that perfect man who is Christ come to full stature."

"I declare and solemnly attest in the Lord that you must no longer live as the pagans do—their minds empty, their understanding darkened.

"They are estranged from a life in God because of their ignorance and their resistance. . . .

"You must lay aside your former way of life and the old self which deteriorates through illusion and desire, and acquire a fresh, spiritual way of thinking.

"You must put on that new man created in God's image, whose justice and holiness are born of truth.

"Be imitators of God as his dear children.

"Follow the way of love, even as Christ loved you.

"Keep careful watch over your conduct.

"Do not act like fools, but like thoughtful men.

"Make the most of the present opportunity, for these are evil times.

"Do not continue in ignorance, but try to discern the will of the Lord."

At a wedding reception recently we got into a discussion about the former rite of confession and the new rites of reconciliation. Two sisters got into a debate—one preferred the old form, one the new. What surprised me is that one sister said that she doesn't receive the sacrament because she has nothing to confess. She was sincere. She just believed that she was OK. Back to Ephesians for her!

GOD'S IMAGE ON EARTH

To say, as Genesis does three times, that man is made to God's image and likeness means that a human being represents God on earth as in ancient times statues of kings represented the king where he could not personally be present. Thus it is not surprising that Christ asks us to be perfect (whole, integral) as his heavenly Father is perfect. Nor is it surprising that already in Leviticus we are told, "You shall love your neighbor as yourself" (19:18).

We are the image of God. That is what we ought to accept and realize in the new self-acceptance movement. And that is how we ought to live. We ought to see ourselves as vice-roys of God, as representing God here on earth. That is why the Bible adds, "Let them have dominion over the fish of the sea, the birds of the air, the cattle, over all the wild animals and every creature that crawls on the earth." Human beings are to take care of and rule God's creation.

I would say that we are part of the team, but I can't stand the term, used so much in business and politics. But we ought to plan our spiritual progress according to the concept, the reality, that we are the *alter ego* of God on earth. It is such a lofty idea that it may scare us, but how foolish of us to lower or degrade ourselves, as we do when we sin, to some position lower.

"The Lord from the earth created man," says Sirach, "and in his own image he made him. . . . He forms men's tongues and eyes and ears, and imparts to them an understanding heart. With wisdom and knowledge he fills them" (17:1, 5-6a). That's where we begin in planning to be perfect, in our program for holiness.

Members of the church, the Dogmatic Constitution on the Church of Vatican Council II tells us, can follow in Christ's footsteps, and, being made holy by Baptism, can "mold themselves in his image, seeking the will of the Father in all things, devoting themselves with all their being to the glory of God and the service of their neighbor" (Art. 40).

Since life is considered a journey, and even the church is called a pilgrim church, we maybe should not be too sur-prised if God on that final confessional day asks us, with the other sheep and goats as audience, "What did you do on Am-trak?"